PLAY-ALONG Swing WITH A LIVE BAND!

Song Background Notes   3

April In Paris   6

Crazy Rhythm   8

Flying Home   11

Honeysuckle Rose   14

I've Heard That Song Before   20

Perdido   17

Satin Doll   22

Stardust   28

'Tain't What You Do
(It's The Way That Cha Do It)   25

Tuxedo Junction   30

CD Track Listing   32

WISE PUBLICATIONS
part of The Music Sales Group
London / New York / Paris / Sydney / Copenhagen / Berlin / Madrid / Tokyo

Published by
Wise Publications
14-15 Berners Street, London W1T 3LJ, UK.

Exclusive Distributors:
Music Sales Limited
Distribution Centre, Newmarket Road, Bury St Edmunds, Suffolk IP33 3YB, UK.
Music Sales Pty Limited
20 Resolution Drive, Caringbah, NSW 2229, Australia.

Order No. AM997579
ISBN 978-1-84938-098-0
This book © Copyright 2009 Wise Publications,
a division of Music Sales Limited.

Unauthorised reproduction of any part of this publication by any means
including photocopying is an infringement of copyright.

Compiled by Nick Crispin
Edited by Oliver Miller
Series Editor: Fiona Bolton
Music arranged by Paul Honey
Music processed by Paul Ewers Music Design
Song Background Notes by Michael Heatley
Cover design by Fresh Lemon & Adela Casacuberta
Cover illustration by Adela Casacuberta
Text photographs courtesy LFI
Printed in the EU

CD recorded, mixed and mastered by Jonas Persson
Flute: Howard McGill
Keyboard: Paul Honey
Bass: Allen Walley
Drums: Chris Baron

Your Guarantee of Quality
As publishers, we strive to produce every book to the highest
commercial standards. This book has been carefully designed
to minimise awkward page turns and to make playing from it
a real pleasure. Particular care has been given to specifying
acid-free, neutral-sized paper made from pulps which have
not been elemental chlorine bleached. This pulp is from farmed
sustainable forests and was produced with special regard for
the environment. Throughout, the printing and binding have
been planned to ensure a sturdy, attractive publication which
should give years of enjoyment. If your copy fails to meet our
high standards, please inform us and we will gladly replace it.

www.musicsales.com

FREE bonus material.
Download band scores and parts to your computer.

Visit www.hybridpublications.com
Registration is free and easy.

Your registration code is: VV110

Song Background Notes

April In Paris
Count Basie

Count Basie, who died in 1984 aged 79, led a big band for nearly half a century and ranked alongside Duke Ellington as the most popular jazzman on the world stage. The lyrical 'April In Paris' was composed in 1932 by Vernon Duke with words by E. Y. 'Yip' Harburg for the Broadway musical *Walk A Little Faster*, but Basie's definitive 1955 interpretation (featuring trumpeter Thad Jones' famous 'Pop Goes The Weasel' solo) won a deserved place in the Grammy Hall of Fame.

Crazy Rhythm
Chet Baker

Although Oklahoma-born trumpeter Chet Baker died in 1988, his music found a fresh audience as a new millennium began thanks to extensive use of his music in the Oscar-nominated movie *The Talented Mr Ripley*. The number 'Crazy Rhythm' first surfaced in 1928 when it was written by Irving Caesar, Joseph Meyer and Roger Wolfe Kahn for the Broadway musical *Here's Howe*. The swinging 32-bar showtune, first recorded by Roger Wolfe Kahn's Orchestra, has since become a jazz standard thanks to Baker and others.

Flying Home
Lionel Hampton

Multi-instrumentalist Lionel Hampton fronted a band longer than any other swing-era legend. Wife Gladys encouraged him to concentrate on the vibraphone, considered a novelty instrument at that time, and with it he created an amalgam of swinging jazz and driving rhythm and blues. 'Flying Home' was his signature tune, composed on his first aeroplane trip in 1939 as he and fellow members of Benny Goodman's band flew from Los Angeles to a gig in Atlantic City on the east coast.

Honeysuckle Rose
Fats Waller

Thomas 'Fats' Waller graduated from accompanying blues legend Bessie Smith, as a teenager, to signing with Victor Records in 1934. By this time the ebullient pianist had formed a partnership with lyricist Andy Razaf, with whom he composed many of his famous tunes including 'Ain't Misbehavin' and this song, 'Honeysuckle Rose'. Introduced as a dance number in the 1929 revue *Load Of Coal* at Connie's Inn in Harlem, it was to be one of his first recordings and was inducted in the Grammy Hall of Fame in 1999.

I've Heard That Song Before
Harry James

One of the finest of all big-band trumpet players, with fine articulation and a genuine ability to stir the audience, trumpeter Harry James was encouraged by Benny Goodman to form his own outfit. The hits followed, including 1942's 'I've Heard That Song Before', penned by Jule Styne and Sammy Cahn. Frank Sinatra covered the song, cementing its status as a swing classic, while James' version of the song, with vocals contributed by Helen Forrest, can be heard in Woody Allen's movie *Hannah And Her Sisters*.

Perdido
Juan Tizol / Duke Ellington

The impact of Edward Kennedy 'Duke' Ellington on the jazz scene spread over six decades as musician, arranger and bandleader, his work reaching beyond the confines of a minority-appeal music. Trombonist Juan Tizol wrote only two tunes with his boss during a 15-year stint with Ellington's band from 1929 but both 'Caravan' and the featured 'Perdido' have become standards, the latter meaning 'lost' in Spanish.

Satin Doll
Duke Ellington / Billy Strayhorn

Duke Ellington's golden era from the late '20s to the mid '40s in which he made his name as both a writer and bandleader, was given a further dimension with the recruitment of pianist/arranger Billy Strayhorn in 1939. The lyrics to 'Satin Doll' were written by Johnny Mercer after the song was already a hit in its instrumental form, Ellington having used it as the closing number at most of his concerts, and it has since been recorded by such illustrious artists as Ella Fitzgerald and Frank Sinatra.

Stardust
Hoagy Carmichael / Artie Shaw

Born in 1899, Hoagland Howard 'Hoagy' Carmichael wrote numbers for artists such as Louis Armstrong and Bing Crosby to perform in movies, but later took cameo roles in films singing the songs he created. Carmichael's classic was 1929's 'Stardust', which he wrote two years earlier; Mitchell Parish added words in May that year, a student having named it because, "It sounded like dust from stars drifting down through the summer sky". Clarinettist Artie Shaw's recording of the tune sold many millions of 78rpm records.

'Tain't What You Do (It's The Way That Cha Do It)
Sy Oliver / Jimmie Lunceford

The combination of bandleader Jimmie Lunceford and arranger Sy Oliver resulted in some memorable music created in just a few late-'30s years. "Tain't What You Do…' was just one of the swing classics they wrote together, exhibiting Oliver's trademarks of, "Two-beat rhythm, stop-time breaks, intricate saxophone choruses and ear-splitting brass explosions". Oliver defected to Tommy Dorsey in 1939, but "Tain't What You Do…' lived on in the hands of Ella Fitzgerald, the Fun Boy Three and many others.

Tuxedo Junction
Erskine Hawkins / Glenn Miller

Though his aeroplane went down in mysterious circumstances in 1944, Glenn Miller's musical legacy continues to fly high today. His trademark sound was the combination of clarinet and four saxes plus the repeated riff that fades away before reappearing. Erskine Hawkins, who wrote 'Tuxedo Junction' was a prominent African-American trumpeter, bandleader and Miller contemporary during the big-band era. He named the number after an area of Birmingham, Alabama.

Glenn Miller

Duke Ellington

Chet Baker

Harry James

Count Basie

Fats Waller

April In Paris
Words & Music by Vernon Duke & E. Y. Harburg

Demo track: Track 02
Backing track: Track 12

© Copyright 1932 Harms Incorporated/Glocca Morra Music Corporation, USA.
Carlin Music Corporation (50%)/Boosey & Hawkes Music Publishers Limited (50%).
All Rights Reserved. International Copyright Secured.

Crazy Rhythm

Words by Irving Caesar
Music by Joseph Meyer & Roger Wolfe Kahn

Demo track: Track 03
Backing track: Track 13

© Copyright 1928 Warner Brothers Incorporated
Warner/Chappell North America Limited (66.66%)/Redwood Music Limited (33.33%).
All Rights Reserved. International Copyright Secured.

8

32 bar ad lib. solo
37 Fmaj9 F6 Fmaj7 F6 B♭13
41 Gm7 C7 C7♭9 Am7 D7♭9 Gm7 C13
45 Fmaj9 F6 Fmaj7 F6 B♭13
49 Gm7 C7 C7♭9 F6 F7
53 Cm7 F7 B♭maj7
57 B♭m7 E♭13 A7♭13 D7♭9 G13 C9
61 Fmaj9 F6 Fmaj7 F6 B♭13
65 Gm7 C7 C7♭9 F6

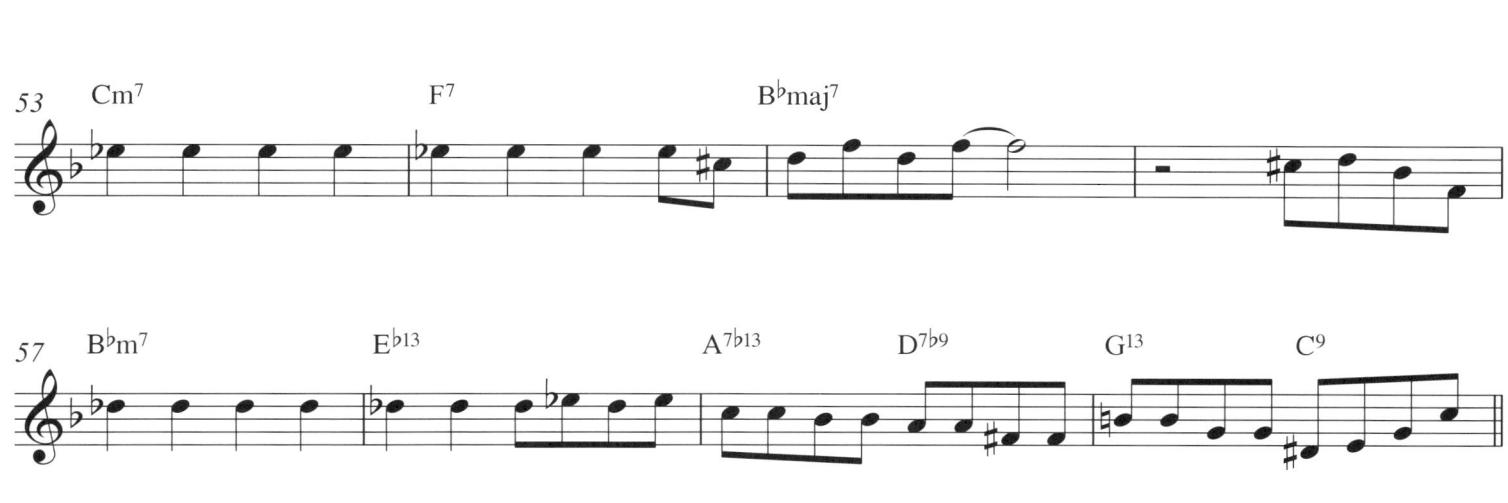

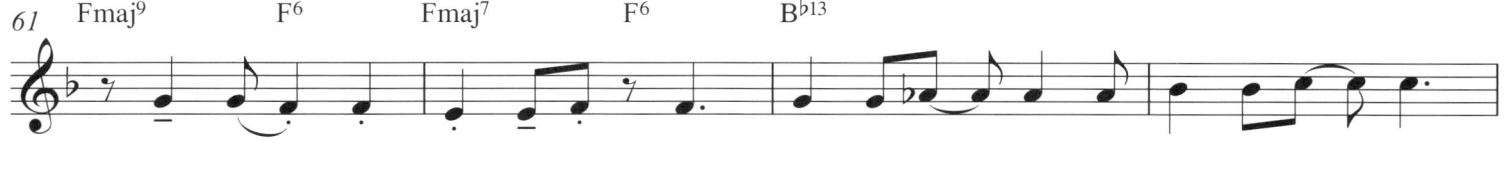

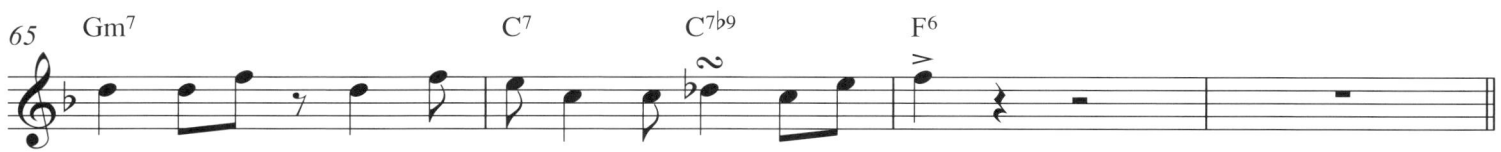

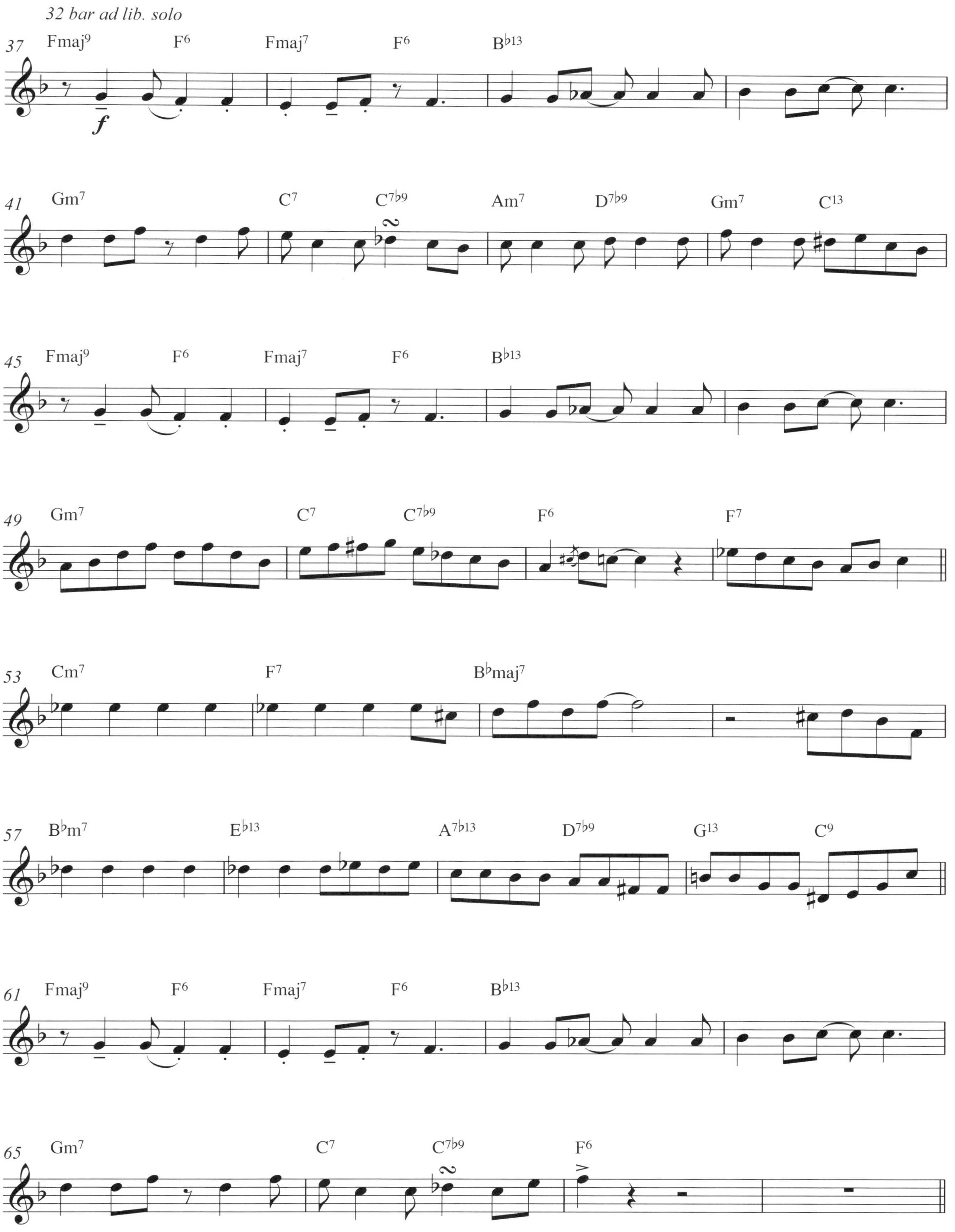

Flying Home
Music by Benny Goodman & Lionel Hampton

Demo track: Track 04
Backing track: Track 14

Honeysuckle Rose

Words by Andy Razaf
Music by Fats Waller

Demo track: Track 05
Backing track: Track 15

Perdido

Words by Ervin Drake & Harry Lenk
Music by Juan Tizol

Demo track: Track 06
Backing track: Track 16

© Copyright 1942 Tempo Music Incorporated, USA.
Campbell Connelly & Company Limited.
All Rights Reserved. International Copyright Secured.

17

I've Heard That Song Before

Words by Sammy Cahn
Music by Jule Styne

Demo track: Track 07
Backing track: Track 17

Satin Doll

Words by Johnny Mercer
Music by Duke Ellington & Billy Strayhorn

Demo track: Track 08
Backing track: Track 18

© Copyright 1953 & 1960 Tempo Music Incorporated, USA.
Campbell Connelly & Company Limited.
All Rights Reserved. International Copyright Secured.

'Tain't What You Do
(It's The Way That Cha Do It)

Demo track: Track 09
Backing track: Track 19

Words & Music by Sy Oliver & James Young

Stardust

Words by Mitchell Parish
Music by Hoagy Carmichael

Demo track: Track 10
Backing track: Track 20

© Copyright 1929 Lawrence Wright Music Company Limited (50%)/Peermusic (UK) Limited (50%).
All Rights Reserved. International Copyright Secured.

28

Tuxedo Junction

Words & Music by Buddy Feyne, Erskine Hawkins, William Johnson & Julian Dash

CD Track Listing

1 Tuning Note

DEMONSTRATION TRACKS

2 **April In Paris** (Duke/Harburg) Carlin Music Corporation/Boosey & Hawkes Music Publishers Limited.

3 **Crazy Rhythm** (Caesar/Meyer/Kahn) Redwood Music Limited/Warner/Chappell North America Limited.

4 **Flying Home** (Goodman/Hampton) Lafleur Music Limited

5 **Honeysuckle Rose** (Razaf/Waller) Redwood Music Limited/IQ Music Limited.

6 **Perdido** (Drake/Lenk/Tizol) Campbell Connelly & Company Limited.

7 **I've Heard That Song Before** (Cahn/Styne) Warner/Chappell Music Limited.

8 **Satin Doll** (Mercer/Ellington/Strayhorn) Campbell Connelly & Company Limited.

9 **'Tain't What You Do (It's The Way That Cha Do It)** (Oliver/Young) Universal/MCA Music Limited.

10 **Stardust** (Parish/Carmichael) Lawrence Wright Music Company Limited/Peermusic (UK) Limited.

11 **Tuxedo Junction** (Feyne/Hawkins/Johnson/Dash) Lafleur Music Limited.

BACKING TRACKS

12 April In Paris

13 Crazy Rhythm

14 Flying Home

15 Honeysuckle Rose

16 Perdido

17 I've Heard That Song Before

18 Satin Doll

19 'Tain't What You Do (It's The Way That Cha Do It)

20 Stardust

21 Tuxedo Junction

To remove your CD from the plastic sleeve, lift the small lip to break the perforations.
Replace the disc after use for convenient storage.